MW01202231

THIRTY MEN WHO
LIVED WITH
CONVICTION

THIRTY MEN WHO
LIVED WITH
CONVICTION

VINCE MILLER

EQUIP PRESS

Colorado Springs

THIRTY MEN WHO
LIVED WITH
CONVICTION

Copyright © 2023 Vince Miller

All rights reserved. No part of this publication may be reproduced, distributed, or transmitted in any form or by any means, without prior written permission.

Published by Equip Press, Colorado Springs, CO

Scripture quotations marked (ESV) are taken from The ESV® Bible (The Holy Bible, English Standard Version®) copyright © 2001 by Crossway, a publishing ministry of Good News Publishers. ESV® Text Edition: 2011. The ESV® text has been reproduced in cooperation with and by permission of Good News Publishers.
Unauthorized reproduction of this publication is prohibited. Used by permission.
All rights reserved.

Scripture quotations marked (KJV) are taken from the King James Bible. Accessed on Bible Gateway at www.BibleGateway.com.

Scripture quotations marked (NASB) are taken from the New American Standard Bible® (NASB), copyright © 1960, 1962, 1963, 1968, 1971, 1972, 1973, 1975, 1977, 1995 by The Lockman Foundation, www.Lockman.org. Used by permission.

Scripture quotations marked (NIV) are taken from the Holy Bible, New International Version. Copyright © 1973, 1978, 1984, 2011 by Biblica, Inc.® Used by permission.
All rights reserved worldwide.

Scripture quotations marked (NKJV) are taken from the New King James Version®.
Copyright © 1982 by Thomas Nelson, Inc. Used by permission. All rights reserved.

Scripture quotations marked (NLT) are taken from the Holy Bible, New Living Translation, copyright © 1996, 2004, 2015 by Tyndale House Foundation. Used by permission of Tyndale House Publishers, Inc., Carol Stream, Illinois 60188. All rights reserved.

Scripture quotations marked (NRSV) are taken from the New Revised Standard Version Bible, copyright © 1989 the Division of Christian Education of the National Council of the Churches of Christ in the United States of America. Used by permission. All rights reserved.

First Edition: 2023
Thirty Men Who Lived with Conviction / Vince Miller
Paperback ISBN: 978-1-958585-42-9

EQUIP PRESS
Colorado Springs

TO: _____

FROM: _____

NOTE: _____

_____

_____

_____

_____

_____

TO:

FROM

NOTE:

TABLE OF CONTENTS

ABOUT VINCE MILLER

Vince Miller was born in Vallejo, California. At twenty, he made a profession of faith while in college and felt a strong, sudden call to work in full-time ministry. After college and graduate school, he invested two decades working with notable ministries like Young Life, InterVarsity Christian Fellowship and in senior leadership within the local church. He currently resides in St. Paul, Minnesota, with his wife, Christina. They have three adult children.

Then in March 2014, he founded Resolute out of his passion for discipleship and leadership development of men. This passion was born out of his personal need for growth. Vince turned everywhere to find a man who would mentor, disciple, and develop him throughout his spiritual life. He often received two answers from well-meaning Christian leaders: *either they did not know what to do in a mentoring relationship, or they did not have the time to do it.* Vince learned that he was not alone. Many Christian men were seeking this type of mentorship relationship. Therefore, he felt compelled to build an organization that would focus on two things: ensuring that men who want to be discipled have the opportunity and that they have real tools to disciple other men.

Vince is an authentic and transparent leader who loves to communicate with men and has a deep passion for God's Word. He has authored several dozen books, and he is the primary content creator of all Resolute content and discipleship materials.

HOW TO USE THIS HANDBOOK

THE METHOD | B.U.I.L.D.

Here is a simple and effective tool for leading your men.

I know this book looks too simple. These short two-page chapters will give you enough discussion for an hour to an hour-and-a-half of great discussion with a group of men. Try it! I promise that a group as small as three or as large as twelve will love it. That's because it is a question-based study that focuses on getting men talking.

But you will notice it gets men talking about one thing: the Bible. Scripture is front and center in this study and every study we do. The questions of each chapter build around this. B.U.I.L.D. is an acrostic that stands for: Begin, Unpack, Inform, Land, and Do.

- **BEGIN** sets the stage for discussion, ensuring that the conversation is headed in the right direction.
- **UNPACK** prompts questions that open up the truth within the text, encouraging deeper exploration.
- **INFORM** guides participants in drawing meaningful insights from the text.
- **LAND** focuses on practical application, helping men discover how they can live out the principles they have learned.
- **DO** motivates men to act, inspiring them to make changes in their lives.

By embracing this approach, we are embarking on a journey to build better men, fostered by meaningful conversations rooted in the Word of God. I invite you to try this study and witness its transformative impact on the lives of the men in your group.

HOW TO LEAD A GROUP

ONE | GET A WINGMAN
Assembling a team is critical. A team should include a pair of leaders who become the "On-Site Hosts" for the experience. We believe working in pairs is by far the most practical approach. Remember, every pilot needs a wingman.

TWO | RECRUIT MEN
Don't stress whether you recruit half a dozen or a hundred, the content will be useful. We have found that the best recruiting success comes from finding men who are hungry to grow spiritually. While the content is suitable for any believer of any age, the best recruit is the one who wants to be there, someone who hungers for the Word of God and occasionally some food as well!

THREE | ENSURE EACH MAN HAS THIS BOOK
Our guides may be purchased in the online store: www.beresolute.org. These are your guides for taking notes, guiding a dialogue in your group, and recording outcomes at the end of every lesson. Handbooks also include other materials for additional development. You will want one for each lesson series.

FOUR | ONLINE RESOURCES FOR THE LEADER
If you have purchased **online video access,** you can view training materials. Here you will find training materials for leading groups of men.

FIVE | MORE MATERIAL FOR MEN

At Resolute, we are not just providing the content. We are inviting you to an experience. Here are other tools you can utilize.

- Need a devotional? Read the Daily Devotional: www. beresolute.org/mdd
- Need prayer? Vince Miller will personally pray for you: www. beresolute.org/prayer-wall
- Need a speaker? Invite Vince Miller to speak: beresolute. org/vince-miller
- Need help as a leader? Contact Vince Miller at vince@ beresolute.org

SIX | REACH OUT TO VINCE MILLER

Contact Vince Miller directly at vince@beresolute.org

AN INTRODUCTION TO THIS STUDY

The Bible is a remarkable collection of stories and teachings that have shaped the lives of countless men throughout history. Within its pages we encounter a diverse cast of real men who, through their unwavering faith and steadfast conviction, left an undeniable mark on the narrative of salvation. In this book we embark on a journey to explore the lives of 30 extraordinary men from the Bible who lived with conviction. From the faith of the patriarchs to the devotion of the prophets, the courage of the apostles to the endurance of the early Church leaders, their stories inspire and challenge us to live with unwavering faith, integrity, and purpose in our own lives.

Each chapter will dive into the lives of these remarkable individuals, examining their unique qualities, key Scriptures, and practical lessons that we can apply to our own journeys of faith. Through their examples we will be encouraged to embrace our calling, trust in God's faithfulness, and live with unwavering conviction in a world that often challenges our faith. Join us as we embark on this enlightening exploration of 30 men who, through their remarkable faith journeys, inspire us to live with conviction amid a changing world.

AN INTRODUCTION
TO THIS STUDY

ADAM

Adam is the first man created by God. He is the progenitor of all humanity and is known for his leadership in the Garden of Eden, his naming of the animals, and his disobedience that led to the fall of humanity.

build

- Give men a few moments to introduce themselves.
- Have one man pray for the group today.

unpack

- Does the world hold a reverent view of human life? Give examples of your position.
- Do men today believe that God interacts with human life? Why or why not?
- If they saw God interact with humanity, do you think this would change their mind about God?

inform

- Read the scripture below out loud. Underline or circle words that have a significant meaning to you.

When no bush of the field was yet in the land and no small plant of the field had yet sprung up—for the Lord God had not caused it to rain on the land, and there was no man to work the ground, and a mist was going up from the land and was watering the whole face of the ground—then the Lord God formed the man of dust from the ground and breathed into his nostrils the breath of life, and the man became a living creature. — Genesis 2:5-7

land

- What details stand out to you within this text?
- Why emphasize using dust as the material for forming the first man?
- Why does God need to breathe into the nostrils of the man for him to become a living creature? Is this important?
- Are there any other details from this moment in Adam's life that stand out to you as important?

do

- How does God care for man as his creation?
- How does this impact your view of God and his care for you?
- How should you live based on this view?
- What one action will you take this week based on this view?

notes

NOAH

Noah is a righteous man who found favor with God in a corrupt and wicked time. He was chosen by God to build an ark to save his family and a remnant of animals during the great flood. He demonstrated unwavering faith and obedience.

build

- Introduce men again. Give attention to any new men in the group.
- Have someone pray for the group today.

unpack

- What are some details you know about Noah?
- Do you believe that a worldwide flood was a loving action by God?
- Do you ever find yourself wanting a fresh start? Why? Share this with the men.

inform

- Read the scripture below out loud. Underline or circle words that have a significant meaning to you.

These are the generations of Noah. Noah was a righteous man, blameless in his generation. Noah walked with God. And Noah had three sons, Shem, Ham, and Japheth. — Genesis 6:9-10

land

- Based on this text, what made Noah unique?
- What do you think it means that Noah "walked with God?"
- Are there any other details from this moment in Noah's life that stand out to you as important?

do

- Who are the generations in your family?
- How have they proved to be righteous or unrighteous?
- What is your vision for your future generations, and what do you need to do make your vision possible?

notes

ABRAM

Abram, later known as Abraham, is a central man in the Bible and is considered the father of many nations. Directed by God he embarked on a journey of faith, he left his homeland and became the recipient of God's covenant promises, including the promise of descendants as numerous as the stars, and the land of Canaan as an inheritance.

build

- Share your high points and low points from last week.
- Have someone pray for the group.

unpack

- If God called you to walk away from it all, would you?
- What if God called you but did not tell you where to go, would you still go?

inform

- Read the scripture below out loud. Underline or circle words that have a significant meaning to you.

Now the Lord said to Abram, "Go from your country and your kindred and your father's house to the land that I will show you. And I will make of you a great nation, and I will bless you and make your name great, so that you will be a blessing. — Genesis 12:1-2

land

- What great things did God promise Abram?
- What did the promise require of Abram?
- What does it sound like to hear God's voice like this?

do

- How can you apply Abram's obedience to God's call to your life?
- What areas of our lives might require us to step out in faith and trust God's guidance, even leaving our comfort zones?
- How can we be a blessing to others, just as God promised to bless Abram?
- How can you use the blessings and resources we have been given to positively impact the lives of those around us?

notes

ISAAC

Isaac, the son of Abraham and Sarah, was a key man in the biblical narrative. He was the child of promise, born in their old age, and was willing to be sacrificed by his father as an act of obedience to God, before being spared at the last moment. Isaac's life exemplifies faith, trust, and the fulfillment of God's covenant promises.

build

- Ask the men if there is anything the group needs to pray for and write the requests down.
- Have someone pray for the group.

unpack

- Have you been afraid of the future at times in your life? If so, share how it felt and how you responded.
- If God appeared to you during a moment like this and told you everything would be okay, would you feel any better?

inform

- Read the scripture below out loud. Underline or circle words that have a significant meaning to you.

And the Lord appeared to him the same night and said, "I am the God of Abraham your father. Fear not, for I am with you and will bless you and multiply your offspring for my servant Abraham's sake." So he built an altar there and called upon the name of the Lord and pitched his tent there. — Genesis 26:24-25

land

- Do you have a family legacy like Isaac's? A father who had great faith, or one who was obedient to God?
- What would you need to do to build a legacy like Abraham did for Isaac?
- What kinds of blessings come from faith and obedience?

do

- How can you cultivate a sense of trust and fearlessness in your life?
- Isaac built an altar and called upon the name of the Lord: how can you acknowledge God's faithfulness and provision in your life?
- Reflecting on the connection between Isaac's blessings and his father's legacy, Abraham, how can you live in a way that honors and continues the spiritual heritage of those who came before you?
- In light of Isaac pitching his tent, how can you establish a sense of stability in your relationship with God?

notes

JACOB

Jacob, also known as Israel, was the son of Isaac and Rebekah, and the grandson of Abraham. He is known for his complex life story, including his deceptive actions to obtain his brother Esau's birthright and blessing, his encounters with God, and his transformation from a self-centered man to a man of faith who wrestled with God and became the father of the twelve tribes of Israel.

build

- Ask the men if there is anyone they know in their life who needs prayer. Write down these prayer requests.
- Have someone pray for the requests as a group.

unpack

- Did you ever have a nickname growing up? What was it? How did you get it, and what was its meaning?
- Do you know the meaning behind your given name? What is it? What does it mean?

inform

- Read the scripture below out loud. Underline or circle words that have a significant meaning to you.

Then he said, "Let me go, for the day has broken." But Jacob said, "I will not let you go unless you bless me." And he said to him, "What is your name?" And he said, "Jacob." Then he said, "Your name shall no longer be called Jacob, but Israel, for you have striven with God and with men, and have prevailed." — Genesis 32:26-28

land

- Who is Jacob wrestling with? (Look it up if you don't know.)
- Quickly look up the meaning of the name "Jacob." Share this with the group.
- What does the name "Israel" mean? (Hint: the meaning is in the text.)
- How does this meaning shape or shift Jacob's identity?
- How does this meaning shape the forward meaning for the people of Israel?

do

- How has your identity changed since your encounter with God?
- How has this identity and encounter with God affected future generations in your life?
- How would you like this to shape future generations?
- What will you do this week to foster this?

notes

JOSEPH

Joseph, the son of Jacob and Rachel, is known for his remarkable story of resilience, faithfulness, and redemption. Despite being sold into slavery by his jealous brothers, Joseph rose to a position of prominence in Egypt through his God-given ability to interpret dreams, ultimately becoming a wise and compassionate leader who saved his family and the land from a severe famine.

build

- Share an injustice that is happening right now in the world that you are concerned about. Write them down.
- Have someone pray for these injustices as a group.

unpack

- Does injustice irritate you? Why, or why not?
- What can be done about these injustices?
- How should Christian men respond?

inform

- Read the scripture below out loud.
  Note any actions or relationships.

His brothers also came and fell down before [Joseph] and said, "Behold, we are your servants." But Joseph said to them, "Do not fear, for am I in the place of God? As for you, you meant evil against me, but God meant it for good, to bring it about that many people should be kept alive, as they are today. So do not fear; I will provide for you and your little ones." Thus he comforted them and spoke kindly to them. — Genesis 50:18-21

land

- If you know the context, why are Joseph's brothers standing before him?
- If you know the story, what is Joseph's present position in Egypt?
- Why would Joseph's brothers be afraid of him? What evil did the brothers do did that they would be concerned about?
- When Joseph had the upper hand, what kind of awareness and strength would be required not to seek vengeance?

do

- Think about the last injustice you suffered. Did you seek vengeance? If you did, what happened? If you did not, why did you choose not to seek revenge, and what happened?
- Which requires more masculine strength: acting in vengeance or withholding vengeance?
- If you are suffering through a present injustice, share this with the group and consider the best path forward with the group based on this text.

notes

MOSES

Moses was a man chosen by God to lead the Israelites out of slavery in Egypt. He performed miraculous signs and received the Ten Commandments on Mount Sinai. He guided the Israelites through the wilderness and towards the Promised Land, leaving a legacy as a lawgiver and prophet.

build

- Share one challenge you are facing at work or in your life. Write it down.
- Have someone pray for these challenges as a group.

unpack

- Have you ever had a moment when you were asked to do something bigger than your present capabilities? What was it?
- How did this moment feel?
- What was the outcome?

inform

- Read the scripture below out loud.
  Note any crucial details in the
  conversation between God and Moses.

But Moses said to God, "Who am I that I should go to Pharaoh and bring the children of Israel out of Egypt?" He said, "But I will be with you, and this shall be the sign for you, that I have sent you: when you have brought the people out of Egypt, you shall serve God on this mountain." Then Moses said to God, "If I come to the people of Israel and say to them, 'The God of your fathers has sent me to you,' and they ask me, 'What is his name?' what shall I say to them?" God said to Moses, "I am who I am." — Exodus 3:11-14

land

- Who is Moses? If you know the context,
  what is about to happen? (If you don't
  know, read back over Exodus 3.)
- What is the relationship between
  Moses and Pharoah? (If you don't know,
  look it up.)
- Why would Moses be concerned about
  the job God was giving him?
- Why would Moses be concerned about
  what the Pharoah and the Israelites are
  going to think?
- At the end of this text, God uses his
  timeless name. Why does God do this?

do

- What impossible situation are you encountering? Do you believe God is bigger than what you are facing?
- What do you need to preach to yourself about God in order to know and believe God is bigger than this situation?
- You may need a brother to speak the truth to you about God through this. Who is the believing brother you will call on and contact this week?

notes

JOSHUA

Joshua, a trusted and courageous leader, succeeded Moses as the one who led the Israelites into the Promised Land. He displayed unwavering faith, leading the conquest of Canaan and allocating the land among the twelve tribes, and he established a strong foundation for the nation of Israel.

build

- Is there someplace you feel like God is not present in your life? Share this without getting into too many details. Write down the response of each man.
- Have someone pray for each man as a group.

unpack

- Share a few more details about this situation where you feel God is not present. What is going on? Why do you feel this way?

inform

- Read the scripture below out loud.
  Underline critical moments and details.

This Book of the Law shall not depart from your mouth, but you shall meditate on it day and night, so that you may be careful to do according to all that is written in it. For then you will make your way prosperous, and then you will have good success. Have I not commanded you? Be strong and courageous. Do not be frightened, and do not be dismayed, for the Lord your God is with you wherever you go. — Joshua 1:8-9

land

- What is the Book of the Law?
- What does it mean when God says it "shall not depart from your mouth"?
- What does it mean to "meditate on it day and night"?
- What is the outcome?
- What type of fortitude does Joshua need to do all the above?

do

- What is convicting about this text?
- What do you need to do to feel more connected to God?

notes

SAMUEL

Samuel was a prophet, priest, and the last judge of Israel. From a young age he heard the voice of God and played a crucial role by anointing and guiding the first two kings of Israel, Saul and David, also in transitioning Israel from a theocracy to a monarchy.

build

- Where in your life do you need to hear from God right now? Try to avoid getting into too many details. (We will discuss this in more detail later.) Write down the response of each man.
- Have someone pray for each man as a group.

unpack

- What do you need specific clarity about?
- What is God not clarifying that you want him to explain?
- Do you think he has spoken, and you have missed what he said?

inform

- Read the scripture below out loud.
  Underline critical events and people.

And the Lord called Samuel again the third time. And he arose and went to Eli and said, "Here I am, for you called me." Then Eli perceived that the Lord was calling the boy. Therefore Eli said to Samuel, "Go, lie down, and if he calls you, you shall say, 'Speak, Lord, for your servant hears.'" So Samuel went and lay down in his place. And the Lord came and stood, calling as at other times, "Samuel! Samuel!" And Samuel said, "Speak, for your servant hears." — 1 Samuel 3:8-10

land

- Samuel heard God three times. Who did Samuel think was speaking?
- Why did God do this three times? Was there a specific response God was looking for?
- How did Eli help Samuel understand what was happening and lead him to the right response?
- Now that Samuel recognizes God's voice, how does he respond the third time this happens?

do

- What do you need to do to hear from God?
- What things might be keeping you from hearing from God?
- How would a believing brother help you hear from God?

notes

DAVID

David, a shepherd boy turned king, is one of the most prominent men in the Bible. Known for his unwavering faith, bravery, and musical talents, David is celebrated as the author of many Psalms and was known as a man after God's own heart. He united the twelve tribes of Israel, established Jerusalem as the capital, and his lineage led to the birth of Jesus Christ.

build

- What is one current spiritual victory?
  Write down the response of each man.
- Have someone pray for the men as a
  group.

unpack

- Is there a place you need a victory?
  Share it.
- What is the victory you want?
- What victory do you think God wants?

inform

- Read the scripture below out loud.
  Underline key moments.

Then David said to the Philistine, "You come to me with a sword and with a spear and with a javelin, but I come to you in the name of the Lord of hosts, the God of the armies of Israel, whom you have defied. This day the Lord will deliver you into my hand, and I will strike you down and cut off your head. And I will give the dead bodies of the host of the Philistines this day to the birds of the air and to the wild beasts of the earth, that all the earth may know that there is a God in Israel, and that all this assembly may know that the Lord saves not with sword and spear. For the battle is the Lord's, and he will give you into our hand." — 1 Samuel 17:45-47

land

- How does David's statement inspire you?
- Who is fighting this battle?
- Who will win the battle?
- In this text, what things does David do in the battle?

do

- How do you think God wants to fight in your battle?
- What are you going to do to get out of his way?

notes

SOLOMON

Solomon, the son of David and Bathsheba, was renowned as a man for his wisdom, wealth, and grandeur. As the third king of Israel, he oversaw the construction of the magnificent temple in Jerusalem, His reign was characterized by peace, prosperity, and the flourishing of wisdom literature, including the book of Proverbs and Ecclesiastes.

build

- What wisdom do you need this week? Have each man share and write it down.
- Have someone pray for wisdom for all the men as a group.

unpack

- Who is a wise man that you know? What wisdom have you gained from him?
- How have you grown in wisdom? Are there certain things you have done to succeed in this?

inform

- Read the scripture below out loud. Underline keywords.

Trust in the Lord with all your heart,
    and do not lean on your own understanding.
In all your ways acknowledge him,
    and he will make straight your paths. — Proverbs 3:5-6

land

- This is a wisdom statement by Solomon, one of the wisest men who ever lived. What does it mean?
- What does it mean to "not lean on your own understanding"?
- What does it mean to "In all your ways acknowledge [the Lord]"?
- What does it mean to "make straight your paths"?

do

- What do you need to do differently to grow in wisdom?
- Is it possible to speed this up a bit?

notes

ELIJAH

Elijah was a powerful and zealous prophet in the Old Testament. He confronted the prophets of Baal, demonstrating the superiority of the true God through a miraculous display of fire, and later experienced a dramatic encounter with God on Mount Horeb. His ministry was marked by boldness, miracles, and a call for repentance in a time of spiritual decline in Israel.

build

- Is there something you have not told the group that you want to get off your chest today?
- Have someone pray for the group.

unpack

- Why do men hesitate or waver?
- Are you hesitating to act in your spiritual life? Over what? And why?

inform

- Read the scripture below out loud. Underline key names.

So Ahab sent to all the people of Israel and gathered the prophets together at Mount Carmel. And Elijah came near to all the people and said, "How long will you go limping between two different opinions? If the Lord is God, follow him; but if Baal, then follow him." And the people did not answer him a word. — 1 Kings 18:20-21

land

- Who are all the characters in this text? List them and describe them. (If you must look them up, do so.)
- What were the two opinions? Were these people spiritually inclusive? How is being inclusive wavering?
- Why do you think the people we silenced by Elijah's comments?
- Why are men like Elijah important?

do

- Do you think, speak, and act like Elijah?
- In what ways could you be more like Elijah?
- How would this be courageous and challenging for you? Are you ready to start the adventure?

notes

ELISHA

Elisha, the successor of Elijah, was a prominent prophet known for his double portion of Elijah's spirit. He performed numerous miracles, including multiplying oil, raising the dead, and healing the sick, while also mentoring and training other prophets. Elisha's ministry demonstrated God's power and faithfulness, leaving a lasting impact on the people of Israel.

build

- What is the best thing that happened to you this last week?
- Have someone pray and praise God's work over the last week.

unpack

- What superpower do you wish you had? Why this one?
- What would be your second choice for a superpower? Why?

inform

- Read the scripture below out loud. Underline keywords, names, and phrases.

When they had crossed, Elijah said to Elisha, "Ask what I shall do for you, before I am taken from you." And Elisha said, "Please let there be a double portion of your spirit on me." And he said, "You have asked a hard thing; yet, if you see me as I am being taken from you, it shall be so for you, but if you do not see me, it shall not be so." And as they still went on and talked, behold, chariots of fire and horses of fire separated the two of them. And Elijah went up by a whirlwind into heaven. And Elisha saw it and he cried, "My father, my father! The chariots of Israel and its horsemen!" And he saw him no more. — 2 Kings 2:9-12

land

- Summarize the story.
- Elisha is the understudy to Elijah. What does he want from his mentor? Why do you think he wants this?
- Explain why Elijah says, "If you see me as I am being taken from you, it shall be so for you, but if you do not see me, it shall not be so."
- How did Elisha respond? Why this way?

do

- Do you have a great and godly older man who speaks into your life? Who is he?
- What things has he shown you about God that makes God greater to you?
- How has he made you a better man?
- If you don't have a godly older man who speaks into your life, is there one you need to ask to do so?

notes

JOB

Job, a righteous and prosperous man, faced unimaginable suffering and loss, becoming a central man in the exploration of human suffering and faith. Despite enduring immense trials, Job remained steadfast in his faith and ultimately witnessed God's restoration and blessings, providing a powerful example of trust and perseverance amid adversity.

build

- Did you mess anything up this last week? Describe it.
- Have someone pray for the men.

unpack

- How do you handle mistakes and sins in your life? What's your first response?
- What would you like to do differently?

inform

- Read the scripture below out loud. Note all the key moments.

Then Job arose and tore his robe and shaved his head and fell on the ground and worshiped. And he said, "Naked I came from my mother's womb, and naked shall I return. The Lord gave, and the Lord has taken away; blessed be the name of the Lord." In all this Job did not sin or charge God with wrong. — Job 1:20-22

land

- Just before this, what happened to Job (Read the first chapter of Job to find out.)
- Just after hearing this tragic news, how did Job respond? What did he do? Could you do this?
- How incredible is this that Job did not sin? Could you do this after losing everything?

do

- Do you worship God in the good times and the bad?
- How would worshipping God in the bad times help?
- Do you need to worship God today? In light of something good or bad?

notes

ISAIAH

Isaiah, often referred to as the "Messianic Prophet," was a major prophet in the Old Testament whose writings spanned over several decades. He proclaimed messages of judgment, restoration, and the coming of the Messiah, presenting a vivid picture of God's sovereignty, justice, and redemption for Israel and the nations.

build

- Was there any point in this last week you felt you heard a nudge from the Lord to do or not do something? Describe it.
- Have someone pray for the group.

unpack

- How do you most hear God's voice? Through scripture, the Spirit, personal convictions, friends, or some other way?
- Do you believe there is a way to hear God's voice more clearly and regularly?

inform

- Read the scripture below out loud.
  Note all the key moments.

And I heard the voice of the Lord saying, "Whom shall I send, and who will go for us?" Then I said, "Here I am! Send me." — Isaiah 6:8

land

- What does Isaiah's enthusiastic response teach us? What can we assume about his relationship with God from this response?
- Why does God ask the question? Does he need to?
- Do you think it's interesting that Isaiah is familiar with the voice of the Lord?

do

- How does Isaiah's response to God's call, "Here I am! Send me." inspire or challenge you in your willingness to respond to God's call in your life?
- Have you ever felt God's calling or prompting to step into a specific role or mission? How did you respond? What were the challenges and blessings that came with it?
- Are there specific areas in your life where you sense God may be calling you to step out in faith and serve Him? How can the group pray for and support you in that journey?

notes

JEREMIAH

Jeremiah, known as the "Weeping Prophet," was called by God to prophesy during a time of great national crisis in Judah. Despite facing opposition and rejection, Jeremiah faithfully proclaimed God's message of judgment, repentance, and hope, providing a profound example of obedience and perseverance in the face of adversity.

build

- What kind of work do you do today? Is this work the right vocation for your talents and abilities?
- Have someone pray for the group.

unpack

- Is a vocation calling different from a spiritual calling? Or are they the same?
- When God calls someone, what does that look or sound like?

inform

- Read the scripture below out loud. Underline any keywords.

Now the word of the Lord came to me, saying, "Before I formed you in the womb I knew you, and before you were born I consecrated you; I appointed you a prophet to the nations." — Jeremiah 1:4-5

land

- How does God knowing and consecrating Jeremiah before his birth impact your understanding of God's plans and purposes for him?
- God only revealed this consecration to Jeremiah once he was ready to send him. Why do you think this was?
- What was the job God consecrated Jeremiah to do?
- What does God say this out loud to him? (Open the chapter in your Bible if you need to and find out why.)

do

- How has God or is God consecrating you?
- What gifts and talents do you have that you need to be using for kingdom purposes?
- What steps do you need to help with to get going?

notes

DANIEL

Daniel, a young Hebrew captive in Babylon, rose to prominence as an interpreter of dreams and visions in the royal court. His unwavering faith in God was exemplified in his refusal to compromise his beliefs. It led to miraculous deliverances and prophetic insights that impacted not only his own life but also the course of empires.

build

- Are you more prone to compromise when the pressure is on or push back?
- Have someone pray for the group.

unpack

- Daniel was put in challenging and potentially compromising situations and was faithful every time. Do you know a man who is like Daniel? How is he like him?

inform

- Read the scripture below out loud.
  Underline any critical moments.

When Daniel knew that the document had been signed, he went to his house where he had windows in his upper chamber open toward Jerusalem. He got down on his knees three times a day and prayed and gave thanks before his God, as he had done previously. — Daniel 6:10

land

- Daniel continues to pray to God even though a decree was signed to prevent this. List some of the values Daniel modeled.
- Was this a new behavior given the decree or an old behavior? What does this tell you about Daniel?
- Why was this decree put into writing? (If you don't know, read Daniel 6:1-9.)

do

- What does Daniel's act of obedience teach us about the importance of worshipping God?
- Are you being pressured to "worship" things other than God in your workplace?
- How do you need to imitate the character of Daniel and take a stand for God?

notes

JONAH

Jonah, a reluctant prophet, was sent by God to deliver a message of warning and repentance to the city of Nineveh. After initially attempting to flee from his divine calling, Jonah experienced God's discipline and ultimately fulfilled his mission, witnessing the city's repentance and God's mercy, highlighting the themes of obedience, repentance, and God's relentless pursuit of humanity.

build

- Share one name of a person who is an unbeliever whom you would love to see come to faith in Jesus. Write down their names.
- Have someone pray for these men in the group.

unpack

- Have you ever refused to do something God wanted you to do? Can you recall what it was? Why did you refuse to do it?
- If given a second chance, do you think you would respond differently? Why?

inform

- Read the scripture below out loud.
  Underline any critical moments.

Then the word of the Lord came to Jonah the second time, saying, "Arise, go to Nineveh, that great city, and call out against it the message that I tell you." So Jonah arose and went to Nineveh, according to the word of the Lord. Now Nineveh was an exceedingly great city, three days' journey in breadth. Jonah began to go into the city, going a day's journey. And he called out, "Yet forty days, and Nineveh shall be overthrown!" And the people of Nineveh believed God. They called for a fast and put on sackcloth, from the greatest of them to the least of them. — Jonah 3:1-5

land

- What did God want Jonah to do?
- Do you know why he refused the first time? (Scan Jonah 1-2 for the answer.)
- What was the message?
- What happened as a result?

do

- Even though Jonah was not obedient the first time, the second time had profound results. What hope does this give you?
- Is there an unbeliever or group of unbelievers that you need to be closer to and be bolder in your faith with? What needs to happen in your heart for you to be less reluctant?

notes

JOHN THE BAPTIST

John the Baptist was a prominent man in the New Testament, known as the forerunner of Jesus Christ. He preached a message of repentance, baptized people in the Jordan River, and played a pivotal role in preparing the way for the ministry of Jesus. It was John who proclaimed Jesus as the Lamb of God who takes away the sin of the world.

build

- What kind of change do you wish you could see today?
- Have someone pray about this as a group.

unpack

- What does the word "repent" mean? (If you don't know, look it up.)
- Share one moment in your life of genuine repentance.

inform

- Read the scripture below out loud. Underline any critical statements and characters.

In those days John the Baptist came preaching in the wilderness of Judea, "Repent, for the kingdom of heaven is at hand." For this is he who was spoken of by the prophet Isaiah when he said,

"The voice of one crying in the wilderness:
'Prepare the way of the Lord;
    make his paths straight.'"

Now John wore a garment of camel's hair and a leather belt around his waist, and his food was locusts and wild honey. Then Jerusalem and all Judea and all the region about the Jordan were going out to him, and they were baptized by him in the river Jordan, confessing their sins.
— Matthew 3:1-6

land

- Who is John, and what did he do?
- Why was his role important?
- Who went out to him? Why the great intrigue?
- What happened as a result?

do

- What do you need to repent?
- How will you take a step this week?

notes

PETER

Peter, also known as Simon Peter, was one of the twelve apostles and a close disciple of Jesus Christ. He was a passionate and impulsive leader who, despite his shortcomings, became a prominent man in the early Christian movement. He witnessed miraculous events, preached the Gospel, and played a key role in the establishment of the early Church.

build

- What blessing have you experienced this last week? Share it and write it down.
- Have someone pray and lift praise to God as a group.

unpack

- Has God revealed anything to you lately? Share it with the group.
- Have you acted on that revelation? If you have, has that action affected you or others?

inform

- Read the scripture below out loud. Underline any critical statements and characters.

Now when Jesus came into the district of Caesarea Philippi, he asked his disciples, "Who do people say that the Son of Man is?" And they said, "Some say John the Baptist, others say Elijah, and others Jeremiah or one of the prophets." He said to them, "But who do you say that I am?" Simon Peter replied, "You are the Christ, the Son of the living God." And Jesus answered him, "Blessed are you, Simon Bar-Jonah! For flesh and blood has not revealed this to you, but my Father who is in heaven. And I tell you, you are Peter, and on this rock I will build my church, and the gates of hell shall not prevail against it. — Matthew 16:13-18

land

- Who are the people in the text?
- Why are people debating about Jesus?
- What does it mean when Jesus says, "For flesh and blood has not revealed this to you, but my Father who is in heaven"?
- Why does Jesus give Peter his nickname?

do

- How could you take a stand for your position and confession about Jesus this week? Is there one thing you could do?

notes

PAUL

Paul, formerly known as Saul, was a highly influential man in the New Testament and one of the most prolific writers of the epistles. Once a persecutor of Christians, he underwent a transformative encounter with Jesus and became a devoted apostle, traveling extensively to spread the Gospel, establish churches, and expound on the theological foundations of the Christian faith. His writings and missionary journeys played a crucial role in the early development and expansion of the early Church.

build

- Did you lose a battle this week or recently? Share it with the group.
- Have someone pray for the men who shared as a group.

unpack

- What did God reveal through the battle you lost?
- How has this changed your view of God, others, or yourself?

inform

- Read the scripture below out loud.
  Underline any critical words.

No, in all these things we are more than conquerors through him who loved us. For I am sure that neither death nor life, nor angels nor rulers, nor things present nor things to come, nor powers, nor height nor depth, nor anything else in all creation, will be able to separate us from the love of God in Christ Jesus our Lord. — Romans 8:37-39

land

- What does it mean to be "more than conquerors"?
- What things cannot separate us from God's love? List them.
- What unique qualities do these things have?
- When you feel defeated in battle, do you think this is important to remember?
- Why does Paul preach this message to the Romans?

do

- How will you preach the Good News that you are "more than a conqueror" this week?
- Is there a moment you anticipate you will need these words? When? Where? State it and then act on it.

notes

BARNABAS

Barnabas, whose name means "Son of Encouragement," was a significant man in the early Christian community. He played a key role in vouching for the apostle Paul, enabling him to join the other disciples and contribute to the spread of the Gospel. Barnabas exemplified generosity, support, and a heart for reconciliation within the Church.

build

- Is there someone who has greatly encouraged you? Name them and share why.
- Have someone pray for those who have encouraged us in this life as a group.

unpack

- Where do you need encouragement right now?
- What kind of encouragement do you need?

inform

- Read the scripture below out loud.
  Underline any critical people or events.

Thus Joseph, who was also called by the apostles Barnabas (which means son of encouragement), a Levite, a native of Cyprus, sold a field that belonged to him and brought the money and laid it at the apostles' feet.
— Acts 4:36-37

land

- Why does Joseph have this nickname?
- Is there anything else Barnabas
  did that was significant in the New
  Testament? (If you don't know, look it
  up.)
- What was encouraging about
  Barnabas's actions at this moment?
  Do you know the significance of this
  moment? (If not, read Acts 4 to find out)
- Do you think this was an easy decision
  for Barnabas? Defend your answer.
- Do you think he gave without expecting
  anything in return?

do

- How do you need encouragement?
- Who needs your encouragement this week?

notes

STEPHEN

Stephen, a man full of faith and the Holy Spirit, was one of the first deacons in the early Church. He boldly proclaimed the Gospel and confronted religious opposition, ultimately becoming the first recorded martyr. His unwavering commitment to Jesus Christ set an example of steadfastness and devotion to the truth.

build

- Do you know someone who is being attacked for their faith?
- Have someone pray for those who are being attacked as a group.

unpack

- Have you ever spoken out about your faith to a hostile audience? Share with the group.
- If not, why not? Would you like to be able to do this? What keeps you from being able to do this?

inform

- Read the scripture below out loud. Underline any important people or events.

And [Stephen] said, "Behold, I see the heavens opened, and the Son of Man standing at the right hand of God." But they cried out with a loud voice and stopped their ears and rushed together at him. Then they cast him out of the city and stoned him. And the witnesses laid down their garments at the feet of a young man named Saul. And as they were stoning Stephen, he called out, "Lord Jesus, receive my spirit." And falling to his knees he cried out with a loud voice, "Lord, do not hold this sin against them." And when he had said this, he fell asleep. — Acts 7:56-60

land

- Acts 7 is one long speech by Stephen, which condemns the religious officials. Do you think Stephen knew this was going to result in a violent reaction?
- Why do you think Stephen got to see the heavens opened?
- Why did the religious officials stone Stephen?
- How is this moment like Jesus's death?
- Do you think this was a glorious or unfortunate closing chapter of Stephen's life?

do

- How would you like to be remembered at the close of your life?
- What changes do you need to make for this to so?

notes

PHILIP

Philip, one of the original twelve apostles, was known for his willingness to follow Jesus and share the good news. He demonstrated a heart for evangelism, as seen in his interactions with the Ethiopian eunuch, and played a significant role in spreading the Gospel message beyond the borders of Israel.

build

- What are you "hearing" from the Lord these days?
- Have someone pray for these as a group.

unpack

- Have you ever heard the Lord distinctly tell you to do something or not do something? Share with the group.
- What does this prompt or voice sound like? Try to describe this.

inform

• Read the scripture below out loud. Underline any important people or events.

Now an angel of the Lord said to Philip, "Rise and go toward the south to the road that goes down from Jerusalem to Gaza." This is a desert place. And he rose and went. And there was an Ethiopian, a eunuch, a court official of Candace, queen of the Ethiopians, who was in charge of all her treasure. He had come to Jerusalem to worship and was returning, seated in his chariot, and he was reading the prophet Isaiah. And the Spirit said to Philip, "Go over and join this chariot." So Philip ran to him and heard him reading Isaiah the prophet and asked, "Do you understand what you are reading?" And he said, "How can I, unless someone guides me?" And he invited Philip to come up and sit with him. — Acts 8:26-31

land

• What are a few highlights from this encounter?
• List the ways Philip and the eunuch are hearing from God. What do you learn from this about how to hear from God?

do

- Is there a situation where you need a voice and direction from God right now?
- Are you ready to ask him to speak?
- Do you think you are willing to listen?

notes

JOHN MARK

John Mark, also known simply as "Mark," was a companion of both Paul and Peter and played a role in the early Christian community. Although he had a rocky start, leaving a missionary journey prematurely, he later became a trusted and valued associate, serving as an assistant to the apostle Peter and eventually authoring the Gospel of Mark, which provides a unique perspective on the life and ministry of Jesus Christ.

build

- What are some small ways older men need to support younger men in the faith today? List them.
- Have someone pray for these needs as a group.

unpack

- Who is a younger man you have mentored?
- What did you say, do, or show him during this time of mentoring?

inform

- Read the scripture below out loud. Underline any important people or events.

So, being sent out by the Holy Spirit, [Barnabas & Paul] went down to Seleucia, and from there they sailed to Cyprus. When they arrived at Salamis, they proclaimed the word of God in the synagogues of the Jews. And they had John to assist them. — Acts 13:4-5

land

- Who are Barnabas and Paul?
- What is John Mark's role?
- Is John Mark's role insignificant just because it's a small notation in this text?
- Why would Barnabas and Saul bring him along?

do

- Is there someone you need to bring along?
- In bringing them along, what will you plan to say, do, or show them?

notes

TIMOTHY

Timothy, a young man and close disciple of the apostle Paul, was entrusted with important responsibilities in the early Church. He received personal instruction and guidance from Paul, became a trusted leader, and served as a representative of Paul, exemplifying faithfulness, dedication, and a passion for the Gospel.

build

- Is there a young man you have known who was very gifted spiritually when he was young? Share some details about him.
- Have someone pray for our young men of faith today.

unpack

- Were you very spiritual when you were younger? Share this with the group.
- Do you feel this would have been different if you had some spiritual men investing in your life?

inform

- Read the scripture below out loud. Underline any important people or events.

Paul came also to Derbe and to Lystra. A disciple was there, named Timothy, the son of a Jewish woman who was a believer, but his father was a Greek. He was well spoken of by the brothers at Lystra and Iconium. Paul wanted Timothy to accompany him, and he took him and circumcised him because of the Jews who were in those places, for they all knew that his father was a Greek. As they went on their way through the cities, they delivered to them for observance the decisions that had been reached by the apostles and elders who were in Jerusalem. So the churches were strengthened in the faith, and they increased in numbers daily. — Acts 16:1-5

land

- Who are Paul and Timothy?
- Why is their relationship important? (If you don't know, you might want to skim 1 & 2 Timothy.)

do

- Is there someone you need to be mentoring or mentored by?
- What do you hope to pass on or learn in this relationship?
- How would this help you even immediately?

notes

SILAS

Silas, also known as "Silvanus," was a prominent companion and fellow worker of the apostle Paul. He accompanied Paul on his missionary journeys, encouraged believers, and was known for his strong faith and commitment to the ministry. He endured hardship and imprisonment for the sake of spreading the Gospel.

build

- What door do you want or need God to open for you today? Write down the responses.
- Have someone pray for these as a group.

unpack

- Is there a door that seems shut and locked to you?
- Do you feel like a prisoner behind this door?
- What needs to happen for the door to be unlocked and opened?

inform

- Read the scripture below out loud. Underline any important people or events.

About midnight Paul and Silas were praying and singing hymns to God, and the prisoners were listening to them, and suddenly there was a great earthquake, so that the foundations of the prison were shaken. And immediately all the doors were opened, and everyone's bonds were unfastened. When the jailer woke and saw that the prison doors were open, he drew his sword and was about to kill himself, supposing that the prisoners had escaped. But Paul cried with a loud voice, "Do not harm yourself, for we are all here." — Acts 16:25-28

land

- In your own words, what is happening here?
- Who unlocked the doors? Why would some view this as only a natural phenomenon?
- Why would God open the doors and the men not exit them?

do

- What do you need to do differently when encountering a closed and locked door?
- Have you thought about how you are going to respond when God opens the door?

notes

APOLLOS

Apollos was a highly skilled and eloquent preacher who played a significant role in the early Church. Although initially lacking a complete understanding of the Gospel, he was fervent in his teaching and, after receiving further instruction from Aquila and Priscilla, became a powerful advocate for Christ, contributing to the growth and edification of the believers.

build

- How would you like to grow spiritually? Write down the responses.
- Have someone pray for these as a group.

unpack

- What needs to happen for you to grow spiritually in the way you mentioned above?
- Is there someone or something that could help you do this?

inform

- Read the scripture below out loud. Underline any important people or events.

Now a Jew named Apollos, a native of Alexandria, came to Ephesus. He was an eloquent man, competent in the Scriptures. He had been instructed in the way of the Lord. And being fervent in spirit, he spoke and taught accurately the things concerning Jesus, though he knew only the baptism of John. He began to speak boldly in the synagogue, but when Priscilla and Aquila heard him, they took him aside and explained to him the way of God more accurately. — Acts 18:24-26

land

- How was Apollos naturally gifted and skilled?
- What had he not been taught?
- Who came alongside Apollos, and what did they do?
- How would this theological coaching complement his natural skills?

do

- How are you gifted and skilled?
- What would it look like to add in some theological coaching? How could this impact others?
- Who could help coach you spiritually?

notes

AQUILA

Aquila, along with his wife Priscilla, was a dedicated couple who played a significant role in the early Church. They were skilled tentmakers and hospitable hosts, and they became influential in instructing and mentoring Apollos in the ways of the Lord, showcasing their commitment to serving and supporting the spread of the Gospel.

build

- Are you going through any changes or transitions in your life or career? Do you feel supported in this?
- Have someone pray for these changes as a group.

unpack

- Name one man who has got behind you in your life.
- What did they do to support you?

inform

- Read the scripture below out loud.
  Underline any important people or
  events.

[Apollos] began to speak boldly in the synagogue, but when Priscilla and Aquila heard him, they took him aside and explained to him the way of God more accurately. And when he wished to cross to Achaia, the brothers encouraged him and wrote to the disciples to welcome him. When he arrived, he greatly helped those who through grace had believed, for he powerfully refuted the Jews in public, showing by the Scriptures that the Christ was Jesus. — Acts 18:26-28

land

- How did Aquila (and his wife Priscilla)
  support Apollos?
- How did they go above and beyond to
  offer this support?
- How did Aquila's show of verbal and
  written support impact the kingdom?

do

- Who is someone who you would like to get behind you?
- Have you asked them? If you haven't asked them, what support would you ask of them?
- How do you see this impacting the kingdom?

notes

TITUS

Titus, a trusted man and co-worker of the apostle Paul, was a valuable leader and representative in the early Church. He played a crucial role in organizing and strengthening the believers in Crete, embodying qualities of integrity, wisdom, and sound doctrine in his ministry and service.

build

- What practical advice did you learn as a young man?
- Have someone pray for the young men of the church as a group.

unpack

- Men, young and old, need practical advice. What practical advice do men need today? List this as a group.
- What on your list is some of the most important practical advice?

inform

- Read the scripture below out loud.
  Underline any advice Paul gives Titus.

But as for you, teach what accords with sound doctrine. Older men are to be sober-minded, dignified, self-controlled, sound in faith, in love, and in steadfastness. Older women likewise are to be reverent in behavior, not slanderers or slaves to much wine. They are to teach what.is good, and so train the young women to love their husbands and children, to be self-controlled, pure, working at home, kind, and submissive to their own husbands, that the word of God may not be reviled. Likewise, urge the younger men to be self-controlled. Show yourself in all respects to be a model of good works, and in your teaching show integrity, dignity, and sound speech that cannot be condemned, so that an opponent may be put to shame, having nothing evil to say about us. — Titus 2:1-8

land

- What practical advice does Titus receive?
- Why is this advice important?
- How will heeding this affect Titus and others?

do

- Are there young men you need to pass spiritual and practical advice off to today? Who are they? What advice do they need?
- How will they be different if they heed this advice?

notes